THEN&NOW

MARBLEHEAD

A day at Devereux Beach *c.* 1900 would not be the same without a bottle of Moxie, some snacks, and plenty of film to photograph your friends and family. The beach, once used by Native Americans as an encampment, was owned in the 17th century by John Devereux. In 1729, the town passed a protective act forbidding the removal of sand, seaweed, and similar material from the area. It was not until 1906, however, that the town acquired the property. (Courtesy Marblehead Historical Society.)

Then & Now
MARBLEHEAD

Sue Ellen Woodcock

ARCADIA

Copyright © 2002, by Sue Ellen Woodcock.
ISBN 0 7385-1018-1

First printed in 2002.

Published by Arcadia Publishing,
an imprint of Tempus Publishing, Inc.
2A Cumberland Street
Charleston, SC 29401

Printed in Great Britain.

Library of Congress Catalog Card Number: 2002101255

For all general information contact Arcadia Publishing at:
Telephone 843-853-2070
Fax 843-853-0044
E-Mail sales@arcadiapublishing.com

For customer service and orders:
Toll-Free 1-888-313-2665

Visit us on the internet at http://www.arcadiapublishing.com

Model yacht racing has been going on at Redd's Pond since 1894, but the first published reference to the sport in town was not until 1930, when Roy Clough was commodore of the Marblehead Model Yacht Club, which was incorporated in 1933 and is still active today. In this photograph, members of the original Midget Yacht Club pose with their vessels on the rocks adjacent to Old Burial Hill c. 1900. (Courtesy Marblehead Historical Society.)

Contents

ACKNOWLEDGMENTS

Poet John Donne wrote that "no man is an island" and, in the making of a book, nothing is truer. I would like to thank the staff of the Marblehead Historical Society for their support in sharing their knowledge and photography collection. I especially thank Pam Peterson (education and exhibition director), who from the start lent her enthusiasm for this project, and Karen MacInnis (curator of collections), my first-string cheerleader who allowed me to borrow the many images used in this book.

A special thank-you also goes to Fred Sullivan, a fourth-grade teacher at the Glover School with more than 30 years of service and a railroad history buff with a penchant for comparing old Marblehead to the Marblehead we know today.

Several people should also be acknowledged for feeding my desire to soak up as much local history about Marblehead as possible: the staff and volunteers of the Marblehead Historical Society; Bette Hunt, historian; Virginia Gamage, historian; Don Doliber, award-winning history teacher and lecturer; William Thompson, a Salem State College history professor; and Warren "Bun" Perry, who popped in to an editing session and ended up staying to share his knowledge. Thanks go to Mary Sullivan and her late husband, Henry "Sully" Sullivan, as well as their daughters Maureen and Judy. Acknowledgment should also go to the late Harold Armstrong, my buddy from the Marblehead Senior Center, who shared wonderful stories about his years at the Tedesco Country Club.

Lastly, I thank my parents, sisters, nephews, and late brother—who have always served as an inspiration to me—and Endicott College and Salem State College for providing the education needed to complete a project such as this.

INTRODUCTION

To the casual observer, the town of Marblehead may not appear to have gone through much change. After all, Glover's Regiment still marches today as it did during the American Revolution. Many men and women still make their living from the sea, and summer visitors still find this quaint New England town an enchanting place to visit. Buildings dating back to early Colonial times in the downtown section persevere, although the use of such buildings has changed to accommodate the needs of the 21st century. Indeed, Marblehead has the greatest concentration of Colonial buildings in the country.

After you live in an area for some time, you do begin to develop an ability to notice change, but it is the natives who notice the most. After all, they were born here, raised here, and are now spending their golden years here. Some Marblehead natives proudly share that they can trace their family roots back 10 generations in this seaside town.

These folks, fondly called Headers (a name given to those who were born in town, either at the former Mary Alley Hospital or in private homes), are the ones who can entertain others for hours with tales of "then and now." They have experienced the changes and are more than adept at telling stories. A once thriving shoe industry is long gone; sailboats easily outnumber the fishing and lobster boats in the harbor; and the unique Marblehead language, which uses the word *whip* as a greeting, is used only by those whose heritage is deeply entrenched in Marblehead's past.

Of course, those who use the word *whip* today know that their mothers considered it a swear word, and using it could mean a bar of soap for dinner. Other unique Marblehead phrases are still heard today, including *down bucket, up for air,* and *rock 'em 'round the corner.* Headers are also good at giving nicknames, such as "Licorice Legs" Blaney, "Pint" Phillips (the milkman), "Pencil" Woodfin, Tom "Teat" Roads (who had diary cows), "Soapy" Waters, "Birdie" Birchmore, "Bucket" Manning, and John "Buzzy" Palmer (the recently retired police chief). Some of the nicknames have stuck so well that you really have to think about what the real names are.

It is the longstanding individualism and spirit of independence that has stood the test of time in this town. Marblehead broke off from Salem in 1648 and was incorporated as a town in 1649. Over the years, the people of Marblehead have proven how resilient they are. After the American Revolution left hundreds of widows and orphans and a crushed fishing industry, the town started rebuilding and fishing once again fed the local economy. However, the fishing fleet was virtually destroyed in the Great Gale of 1846. Today, a monument to those men and boys lost stands in Old Burial Hill, overlooking the ocean.

Residents also proved as early as 1636 that they could build some of the finest ships around. Since then, Marblehead has turned out schooners, fishing vessels, and sailboats. Marblehead even claims to be the birthplace of the American navy, since it was the Marblehead men of Glover's Regiment who sailed the *Hannah* (also owned by Marbleheaders) for Gen. George Washington in 1775. During the War of 1812, the USS *Constitution* sought refuge in the harbor from British ships. Marblehead men proudly defended Old Ironsides, an amazing vessel that has visited the town as recently as 1997. Headers have always remained strong. The town's shoe industry helped pull the economy together after the Great Gale of 1846, but devastation struck again with fires in 1877 and in 1888, wiping out a large portion of the town as we know it today. Once again, the sea helped turn the town around. With the growth of the sailing and boating industry during the 20th century, Marblehead became a draw as a summer resort and as a community suited for raising a family.

It is no wonder that residents and tourists alike are drawn to Marblehead, surrounded by history and the Atlantic Ocean. Whether you spend a summer day at Devereux Beach, sail out of the harbor, or haul lobster traps and fishing lines, there is history all around. You would be hard pressed to find someone willing to leave it all for a lesser community. As you thumb through these pages, rediscover the lure of the sea and the history that in some places seems to have stood still. (Courtesy Marblehead Historical Society.)

Chapter 1

BY THE SEA

Devereux Beach has always drawn a summer crowd. Even in the 1930s and 1940s, the beach parking lot was jammed with automobiles. The beach featured such attractions as Usher's Camps (from the 1920s to the 1960s), Timmie's (owned by Timmy Cahill from the 1930s to the 1950s), and the present-day Flynnie's. (Courtesy Marblehead Historical Society.)

Gerry Island, as viewed by Marblehead photographer Fred Litchman in the 1930s, no longer has buildings on it, but the island is still accessible at low tide and the waters around it serve as a fertile ground for lobsters. (Courtesy Marblehead Historical Society.)

LITCHMAN PHOTO

6.187.14

The lazy, hazy days of summer on Tinker's Island come to an end on September 23, 1906. Tinker's Island, named for the abundance of tinker mackerel off its shores, has been a haven of summer vacationers since the mid-1800s. Once considered part of Marblehead, it was claimed by Salem for taxes in 1969. Today, the island can be viewed from Devereux Beach or from several private homes on Marblehead Neck. (Courtesy Marblehead Historical Society.)

The old Marblehead lobsterman known as Mr. Standley (below) is pictured with his shanty, which overlooked Gerry Island in Little Harbor. As in the early 20th century, shanties can still be found off Fort Beach Way. (Courtesy Marblehead Historical Society.)

Frank Gilbert (left), Skatchey Gilbert (center), and an unidentified man work on a lobster trap at Transportation Wharf *c.* 1900. The old transportation building, once a vital part of the salt-trade industry, still stands today. (Courtesy Marblehead Historical Society.)

The Portland Storm of 1898 slammed fishing vessels and sailboats into the causeway to Marblehead Neck. It was the worst nor'easter since 1851. The causeway was built *c.* 1870, providing new access for people who wished to camp on Marblehead Neck. (Courtesy Fred Sullivan.)

The first lighthouse in town (upper left) was built at Chandler Hovey Park on Marblehead Neck in 1838. A new lighthouse (lower left) was built *c.* 1900 and is shown with the lighthouse keeper's house, which existed until 1957. The light tower was built in 1895 and began working in 1896. Eight lighthouse keepers, including one woman, worked the light until it was automated in 1960. A gangplank down to the sea (below) was still used on the harbor side. The mounting holes for the gangplank can still be seen. Today, the light tower (right) still shines its unique green light for sailors entering the harbor to see. (Left and below, courtesy Marblehead Historical Society; right, courtesy Fred Sullivan.)

A view of Little Harbor from Fort Sewall shows where today's Marblehead Lobster Company is, as well as Gerry Island (right) and Brown's Island (background). At one time, America's Cup champion Ted Hood also had his sail operation at Little Harbor. (Courtesy Fred Sullivan.)

In the late 1800s and early 1900s, Marblehead Neck was the site of several hotels and inns (below). Photographer Fred Litchman caught this view in 1910. The Oceanside can be seen near the site of the lighthouse. New homes built on or near the site today (right) reflect a more contemporary flair on the outside. (Courtesy Fred Sullivan.)

The original Adams House, built in 1908 by John T. Adams on Front Street at Fort Beach, is a fond memory for many. It is shown *c.* 1910 as people would have seen it on the way to Fort Sewall. Pictured are Edgar Rich (left, sitting on the step of the Adams House), and Howard Magee (right, sitting). The others are George Eastland, Henry Magee, George Snow, Bill Howe, Ernest Howe, and Anabelle Howe. (Above, Courtesy Marblehead Historical Society; left, courtesy Fred Sullivan.)

Two postcards show the Adams House in the early 20th century. The house can still be seen, and the street is referred to as Fort Beach Drive. This view, more so than any other site in town, has become a favorite for postcards. (Courtesy Fred Sullivan.)

Seen from Fountain Park across Little Harbor, the Fort Sewall area sits quietly with few houses and Brown Brothers Boatworks. The photograph (above) was taken by photographer Willard Jackson, who documented life around the sea. (Courtesy Marblehead Historical Society.)

In the 1940s, a group of men seems to have gone fishing for an elusive airplane out of Marblehead Harbor near Commercial Street wharf. It is unknown if it is a Burgess aircraft, but the harbor is a place for all sorts of craft, from sailboats to fishing vessels. (Courtesy Marblehead Historical Society.)

The *Watertown* in 1892 was one of several passenger steamers owned by the Boston, Lynn and Salem Steamship Company. It caught fire and burned near Revere after being in use for only two years. The ship, which cost about $50,000 to build, was 135 feet long and had a beam of almost 30 feet. Today, besides seeing a lobster boat pull up to a dock, there is a good chance of seeing a celebrity pull up in a sailboat. (Courtesy Marblehead Historical Society.)

Marbleheaders, who have always had a good Puritan work ethic, dove headlong into the industrial revolution. In this 1929 photograph, local women work the switchboard at the telephone exchange on Pleasant Street near today's Riptide Lounge. Telephone numbers at the time were short and to the point, such as Neptune 3892. (Courtesy Marblehead Historical Society.)

Chapter 2

AT WORK

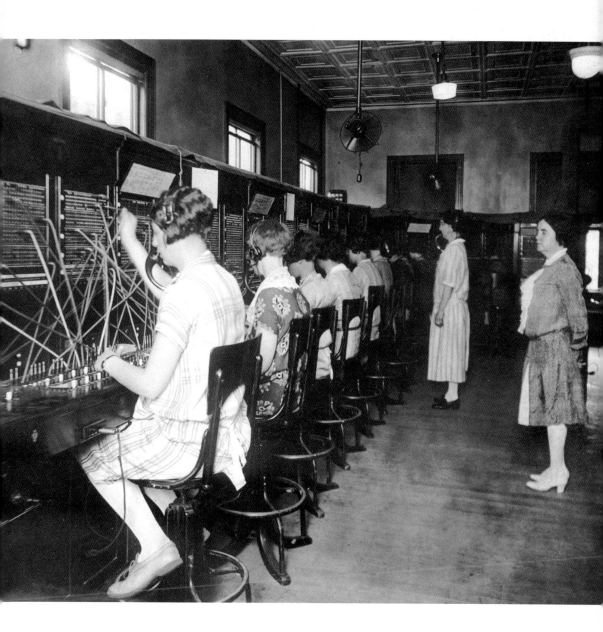

Shoemaking on the North Shore was a prominent industry in the mid-1800s. Marblehead wanted to compete with cities such as Lynn, Peabody, Salem, Haverhill, and Taunton. Until 1888, the Marblehead shoe industry played a vital part in the town's economy, employing more than 2,000 people (many of them young women from Nova Scotia) and exporting fishermen's boots, as well as fine shoes for women and children. One factory saved from the fires was the Association Shoe Factory on Green Street, which occupied two buildings. One of the buildings burned in the 1930s. The second was later razed, and the site is now occupied by single-family homes. (Courtesy Marblehead Historical Society.)

In May 1907, the Central Fire Station was well rooted on School Street. Posing with the firefighting apparatus are, from left to right, the following: (front row) John Dennis, Emery Graves, John Patey, William A. Fader, Charles H. Bartlett, Benjamin W. Woodfin Jr., Arthur Adams, John A. Martin, and chief engineer Frank Wadden; (back row) Joseph Glass, Herbert Bartlett, and Benjamin Holden (driver). The horses are Stronghorse (left), the strongest the department had up to that time, and Bay Horse. Today, the building is used by a community theater group and the Central Fire Station can now be found on Pleasant Street, where it houses bright-red fire engines instead of a horse and wagon. (Courtesy Marblehead Historical Society.)

Fire Chief John T. Oliver (right) is shown in the 1940s. Today, Barry Dixey (below, left) holds that position. Dixey followed Charles Maurais (below, right), who served as chief from 1987 to 1999, and Ed Creighton (below, center), who served from 1962 to 1987. The first permanent fire department was established after the 1888 fire. (Right, courtesy Marblehead Historical Society; below, courtesy Barry Dixey.)

In January 1996, Ray Orne (left) tries to shovel out his business, Litchman & Orne Offset Printing, located on Washington Street. His father, Fred Orne, was also a photographer. He was a partner with Fred Litchman (above center), one of the better-known Marblehead photographers *c.* 1900. Litchman stands with his hand on the post in front of his first business location, on State Street. Savvy observers will recognize it as the building that Maddie's is in today. (Above, courtesy Marblehead Historical Society; left, courtesy Judy Anderson.)

The Burgess flying boat was created for the U.S. Navy. A plaque in a small park located off Gregory Street and Redstone Lane (near the Marblehead Electric Light Department on Commercial Street) commemorates the site where Lt. Alfred Cunningham of the U.S. Marines soloed the Burgess-Dunne hydroplane on August 1, 1912. (Courtesy Marblehead Historical Society.)

The exterior view of the Burgess Aircraft Factory (upper left) was taken from the harbor by photographer Fred Litchman. W. Starling Burgess began laying the foundation at Redstone Cove in Marblehead Harbor for the creation of a seaplane in 1904. In 1910, the *Flying Fish* took a short flight at Chebaco Lake in Hamilton and Plum Island. Two years later, a more successful flight in Marblehead Harbor made Marblehead the birthplace of marine aviation. The operation grew to 800 employees during World War I with a government contract and turned out eight planes a day. Later, the factory was moved to Little Harbor when Burgess teamed up with English designer I. W. Dunne to create Burgess–Dunne. It burned to the ground on November 7, 1918. Inside the factory (lower left), workers in June 1917 build on wings for hydroplanes contracted by the army and navy. In 1918, a group (above) shows off a chassis built for the navy's Class C airships. The craft was 40 feet long, 5 feet deep, and was known as the Zep. (Courtesy Marblehead Historical Society.)

Marbleheaders love their news, either in print form or the kind found on the street. Jack Riley (above) gets the *Boston Herald* delivery wagon ready outside Phil Woodfin's barn on State Street. The first newspaper in Marblehead was the *Marblehead Register,* issued in March 1830. Today, the *Marblehead Reporter,* first published in 1964, is the local weekly newspaper. Staff members (left) include, from left to right, George Derringer, reporter; Fraffie Welch, columnist; and Kris Olson, editor. Today the same company that owns the *Boston Herald* owns the *Marblehead Reporter.* (Courtesy Marblehead Historical Society.)

The *Boston Express* office *c.* 1910 (below) graced the corner of School and Pleasant Streets. Pictured, from left two right with two unidentified boys, are Elbridge Cloutman, the driver; Bill Riley, the bookkeeper for Woodfin Express; and Anne Hourihan, also a bookkeeper. The building was owned by Ed Lefavour and was used as a shoe factory. Prior to that, it was owned John Frank and located on Abbott Court. It was moved to its current location in 1960 and was the site of Warwick Lunch, the Riptide Lounge, and Mayflower Cleaners. Today, the Riptide Lounge, Supersub, and Howard's can be found there. (Courtesy Marblehead Historical Society.)

Today, Howard's newsstand (left) sits on the corner of School and Pleasant Streets. Years ago, around the corner, a group (above) picks up some supplies from Arthur J. Sanford's plumbing shop on School Street. The building next door had also been Brown's Hardware Store and Murphy's Hardware. (Courtesy Marblehead Historical Society.)

The Gilbert & Cole Company (below), a former coal supplier on Bessom Street, was known as the "coal pocket." It burned in the 1950s. Today, looking more like a house (right), the company is a supplier of building materials and can be found on the same site. (Courtesy Fred Sullivan.)

Once known as Love's filling station, the Mobil gas station (left) is now owned by Phil Cash Jr. This service station has been in existence on Atlantic Avenue since cars first came to Marblehead. Note the special "Winter Mobilgas" (above) available at the pump. (Courtesy Fred Sullivan.)

Marblehead is a community full of recreational activities, including sailing, softball, youth sports, competitive badminton at the Gut & Feathers Club, and golf at the Tedesco Country Club. Of course, it is also a great community for just relaxing at an inn or visiting a favorite restaurant. In this view, young Mary Bridge (left) and her friend Helen Paine, daughter of banker Everett Paine, stop by Abbot Hall with their buggy, pulled by Bridge's pony Pinky. (Courtesy Marblehead Historical Society.)

Chapter 3

TIME FOR
PLAY

The Marblehead Athletic Association plays its baseball games at Seaside Park, just as baseball teams do today. Pictured here is the 1916–1917 team. Pictured, from left to right, are George Kelley, Lewis Sullivan, Buddy Cochran, Hep Burdett, "Stuffy" McGuines, ? Mahoney, Lenny Burdett, Stocker Kelley, Chick Davies, Burt

Humphrey (president), Ross Murphy, Billy Bowles, Marty Donovan, Joe Reynolds, Allen Weed, Mike Grody, and Robert Hanson (treasurer). (Courtesy Marblehead Historical Society.)

The 2000 Marblehead High School baseball team is shown with coach Dick Newton at Seaside Park on Atlantic Avenue, where home games are still played. (Courtesy Pam Peterson.)

The photograph of a football game at Seaside Park (below) was taken in 1922 from Gerry Street by photographer Fred Litchman. In 1987, police headquarters was moved across from Seaside Park, and the Catholic church now has a parking lot on the left. While baseball and field hockey are still played at Seaside Park, football is played behind the middle school and will soon be played behind the new high school on Humphrey Street. (Courtesy Marblehead Historical Society.)

Basketball was one of the first sports that girls were allowed to play at many schools across the United States. This 1927 Marblehead High School team, coached by a Mrs. Stiles, sported baggy bloomers, socks to fully cover the legs, and high-top sneakers worn only for playing sports. Today, the Marblehead Magicians girls' basketball team dresses the same as the boys' team and players even might wear their sneakers to class. (Courtesy Marblehead Historical Society.)

The Tedesco Country Club is named for the barque *Tedesco,* which sank off Little's Point in Swampscott. The club has been a fixture at one entrance of Marblehead for almost 100 years, with the first clubhouse being built in 1904. Known for its golf course, the club also once had a badminton court. Suffering through three fires, the current clubhouse was built in 1953. Today, the club sports lush greens in both Marblehead and Swampscott. (Courtesy Marblehead Historical Society.)

The General Glover Restaurant —bearing the name of Brig. Gen. John Glover of Marblehead, who rowed Pres. George Washington across the Delaware River—is just down the street from the Tedesco Country Club on the Marblehead-Swampscott line. The land on the site was once owned by John Glover. The restaurant, now owned by restaurateur Anthony Athanas and his sons, closed in 1999. (Courtesy Marblehead Historical Society.)

This Marblehead police officer (below) shows off his Indian motorized bicycle, acquired by the department as one of the first motorcycles. The man, identified only as Mr. Lillibridge, posed for photographer Fred Litchman sometime in the 1940s in front of the steps at the Old Town House. (Courtesy Fred Sullivan.)

Nothing gets the crowd going like a parade, and no one could grab the audience's attention better than the Okommakamesit Volunteer Firemen's Association bagpipe band in the 1960s (above). The band was started in the early 1900s to help raise money for the war effort. Note the Miller Ford dealership. At the same location today (left) is Miller Plaza, which includes a coffee shop, bank, and convenience store. (Courtesy Fred Sullivan.)

There was a time when it was considered harmless for youngsters to play with guns, just like these boys (below) did in the early 1900s as members of the Junior Home Guard at Bank Square. The organization is now gone, but the buildings at Bank Square remain. (Courtesy Fred Sullivan.)

Goldthwait Beach, right next to Devereux Beach, has been covered with small rocks for decades. In the early 1900s, photographer Fred Litchman captured these folks (above) relaxing by the shore. (Courtesy Fred Sullivan.)

The Pleon Yacht Club, for sailors under the age of 21, was formed in 1887 by a group of young boys interested in the sport of sailing. The club, whose first commodore was Arthur Goodwin Wood, is still going strong, with the red-and-blue pennant with a white star still identifying it. (Courtesy Fred Sullivan.)

The Eastern Yacht Club, on the harbor side of Marblehead Neck, was formed in 1870. The first clubhouse was built in 1881. Shown in the early photograph (above), the club was known as one of the largest and richest in New England. Every evening of the summer, a cannon fired from the club heralds the exact moment the sun sets. (Courtesy Fred Sullivan.)

Not far away is the Corinthian Yacht Club, the first club that boaters see as they enter the harbor. It was founded in 1885 by a group led by C.H.W. Foster and Benjamin W. Crowninshield. Today, the club even has a swimming pool for its members and their guests. (Courtesy Fred Sullivan.)

The Nanepashemet Hotel (above) was located on the corner of Nanepashemet Street and Ocean Avenue on Marblehead Neck. The hotel was built in 1881 by Robert C. Bridge and opened for business in 1882. It burned in 1914. Today, houses cover the same location. (Courtesy Fred Sullivan.)

After rebuilding from the 1877 fire, a second big fire struck Marblehead in the same area in 1888 during the Christmas holiday. The devastation consumed the area around Pleasant Street. Standing strong in the background is Abbot Hall. The fire began on Christmas Eve with an explosion at 10:00 p.m. As a result of the fire, 50 significant buildings were lost, and 2,000 employees lost their jobs. The rebuilding after this fire certainly shaped the areas as they are today along Pleasant Street and streets around it. (Courtesy Marblehead Historical Society.)

Chapter 4

OUR
EVOLVING
TOWN

As seen from Crocker Park, Abbot Hall has served as a beacon since it was constructed in 1876–1877. Benjamin Abbot bequeathed $100,000 to construct a building named after him to be used by the town. The building reaches 164 feet up, including the weathervane. Today, it holds several town offices, as well as Archibald Willard's *Spirit of '76* painting. (Courtesy Fred Sullivan.)

Atlantic Avenue in the early 20th century (below) included many two- and three-story buildings. The view from atop Abbot Hall shows the old Catholic church on the hill to the right. Today, the avenue is dotted with shops and eateries and is one of the main roads leading out of town toward Swampscott and, eventually, Boston. (Courtesy Fred Sullivan.)

57

Viewed from Skinner's Head, where Glover Landing stands today, Abbot Hall stands tall over the town. Gregory Street and Mason's Rocks can be seen in the early-1950s picture (above). (Courtesy Marblehead Historical Society.)

The Sailors' and Soldiers' Monument was moved from the junction of Elm, Green, and Mugford Streets to the park at the corner of Pleasant and Essex Streets. The move began on May 2, 1913, and ended on May 9, 1913. Dedicated on July 4, 1876, the monument is in memory of soldiers who served in the Revolutionary War, the War of 1812, and the Civil War. (Courtesy Marblehead Historical Society.)

The Okommakamesit Volunteer Firemen's Association building, at the intersection of Washington and Middle Streets, is shown c. 1950 (above), when wine-glass elms still enhanced the landscape. The building today houses the Okommakamesit hand engine. The town has had a hand engine since 1751. Today, the engine is used in competition at musters around New England. (Courtesy Marblehead Historical Society.)

The Gregory Building is pictured *c.* 1900 (below) and today. The site once occupied by Gregory's Pharmacy is now Tony's Pizza. The old painted Coca-Cola sign on the side of the building has faded but can still be seen today. The building is a good example of the type of construction mandated after the 1888 fire. The selectmen ordered that all downtown buildings be masonry. (Courtesy Marblehead Historical Society.)

As shown *c.* 1900 (above), the Unitarian church on Mugford Street was next to the old Martin House. The first church building was built in 1715 and burned in October 1910. It was rebuilt in 1911. The first congregation was formed from members who once belonged to the Second Congregational Church. (Courtesy Marblehead Historical Society.)

St. Stephen's Methodist–Episcopal Church was first on Summer Street near Rockaway Street. Today, condominiums occupy the site. St. Michael's Episcopal Church, at the other end of Summer Street, was built in 1714. It was here, after reading the Declaration of Independence, that locals entered the closed church, tore down the royal coat of arms, and rang the church bell until it cracked. Paul Revere was the man who recast the bell and proudly left his stamp on it. (Courtesy Marblehead Historical Society.)

The cornerstone for the new Star of the Sea Catholic Church (below) was laid in 1928 on Atlantic Avenue across from Seaside Park. Earlier, the church was located high on Prospect Hill (Rowland Street), where it was built in 1876. Today, there are apartments in its place. (Courtesy Fred Sullivan.)

Catholic Church, Marblehead, Mass.

Old North Congregational Church was formed in 1635, and its church was built in 1825 on Washington Street. The view with the parsonage (right) was taken on a June morning in the 1930s. The present-day view (below) shows the back of the church as seen from High Street, where the parsonage used to be. (Courtesy Marblehead Historical Society.)

The golden era of summer hotels included the Hotel Rockmere (above), as seen from Crocker Park. Built in 1901, the establishment had a nautical theme, which included the staff's dressing like sailors. In 1965, the town's first condominium development, Glover Landing (left) was built at the site. (Courtesy Fred Sullivan.)

Sheep from the Sorosis Farms at Wyman's Cove loved the rocky, hilly landscape used for grazing. The farm was a venture taken on by shoe manufacturer Alexander Little, who wanted to offer employees at his Lynn factory a chance to purchase farm-related material at cost. He purchased 10 percent of Marblehead's land to do so. The farm also had buildings at Tent's Corner, where the new 2002 high school is to be located. The sheep building was at the corner of Shorewood Road. The farm closed in 1934 after it went bankrupt. (Courtesy Fred Sullivan.)

The Hills and Valleys on Sorosis Farms provide Ideal Conditions for Sheep Raising

Flooding has been a longtime complaint in the area of Chestnut and Central Streets. To this day, crews are working on a permanent solution to the problem. The March 1914 flood (above), called the Great Shipyard Flood, was weathered by a few good souls in a rowboat. (Courtesy Marblehead Historical Society.)

Gathering at John T. Adams's house near Fort Sewall between 1925 and 1930 are, (below) from left to right, the following: (front row) James Magee, ? Perry, Charles Rogers, and John Hennesey; (back row) John T. Adams, Clint Foss, William Merritt, Elbridge Girdler, and Robert Knight. The house still stands today. (Courtesy Marblehead Historical Society.)

The Adams House Restaurant (upper left), built in 1908 by the former fire department chief and restaurateur John T. Adams, is located near Fort Beach. Steps away was the Pirate House (lower left), where pirates are said to have come ashore at Lovis Cove and stored possessions. John T. Adams's house can be seen across the street. Just a stone's throw from the Adams House is Fort Sewall. Built on Gale's Head in 1742, Fort Sewall was named for Chief Justice Samuel Sewall of Marblehead. It was first used as a defense agent against French cruisers. The USS *Constitution* sought the refuge of the fort in 1814, when it was chased by the HMS *Tenedos* and HMS *Endymion*. The earthen fort was also used in the Spanish-American War for several months in 1898. (Courtesy Marblehead Historical Society.)

When the Eastern Railroad branch extended its service from Lynn to Marblehead in the fall of 1871, depots were built at Clifton (shown here) and Devereux, adding to the two stations in Swampscott at Beach Bluff and Phillips Beach. (Courtesy Fred Sullivan.)

The Marblehead train station on Pleasant Street (below) was one of four built on the site. The first was built in 1839, when the Eastern Railroad offered its service on a transportation line once used by stagecoaches. Today, the National Grand Bank (right), named for the great fishing bank off the coast, makes its home on the same spot. (Courtesy Fred Sullivan.)

The Goss-Osborne Building was built in 1888 at the corner of Pleasant and School Streets. Frank Osborne, son of owner F. Norris Osborne, is standing to the far right (above) in the 1930s. (Courtesy Marblehead Historical Society.)

The George W. Grader building, known as Moses Maverick Square, was built in 1885 on Pleasant Street. Shoe store owner Sam Lampkin is looking in his shop window (below). A portion of the building, now with shops and offices, was used in 2001 to film *Hello, Good-bye*, a Dustin Hoffman movie. (Courtesy Marblehead Historical Society.)

Horace Cloon's furniture store (above), stands on the corner of Washington and State Streets *c.* 1900. Note the gas street lamp (used starting in 1854) and the sign to the steam ferry at the State Street landing. Today, the building houses Hector's Pup (a toy store) and a gallery. (Courtesy Marblehead Historical Society.)

Wheeler's Farm Produce (below) once graced the pointed corner at Tedesco, Humphrey, and Maple Streets. In this view from the 1930s or 1940s, Wheeler's pumpkin patch was at the right rear of the building. (Courtesy Fred Sullivan.)

The Chapel Hill area of Marblehead started with a real estate developer. The sales office was located behind what is now St. Andrew's Episcopal Church, on Lafayette Street. NRA (above) stands for the National Recovery Act, which helped lift people out of the Great Depression. (Courtesy Marblehead Historical Society.)

From atop Leggs Hill, the Forest River and Salem Harbor are clearly seen, but *c.* 1900 (below), the Chadwick Lead Mills also graced the landscape. History has it that a group from Plymouth found one of the Great Forts of Nanepashemet in Marblehead near the Forest River and Leggs Hill. (Courtesy Fred Sullivan.)

Leggs Hill Road off Tedesco Street was originally known as Old Salem Road, as shown in the 1940s. The road, which abuts Salem, has been built up over the years and still has open space ripe for development. (Courtesy Marblehead Historical Society.)

In each and every town, there are
people who leave a mark by their deeds
or inventions or in having a place named
after them. Marblehead is no different. It
has a long tradition of men and women
making a difference. As photographer
Fred Litchman captured in 1898, dozens
of men answered the call to serve in the
Spanish-American War. Troops lined up at
the Boston & Maine station on Pleasant
Street, ready to head to Boston to begin
their journey. (Courtesy Marblehead
Historical Society.)

Chapter 5

LEAVING
A MARK

The Old Town House, built in 1727 in Market Square, has served many functions over the years, including being the gathering point for soldiers and veterans alike. Going off to war *c.* 1917, soldiers and their families gather in front of the historic building (upper left). In 1931, veterans of the Civil War gather (lower left). The building has also served as the town's police station and the Mugford Street side of it as a volunteer firemen's association called Liberty Hose (below). A Grand Army of the Republic museum is now housed on the second floor. (Courtesy Marblehead Historical Society.)

Troops serving in the Spanish-American War were well fed by men like these in the cook house at an encampment at Fort Sewall. In 1898, the fort was used by the military for the last time. The Spanish-American War lasted only a few months, from April to August. Encampments were set up to the left of the bowl area. (Courtesy Marblehead Historical Society.)

Several men from Marblehead served as chaplains during World War I. Lyman Rollins, the rector at St. Michael's Episcopal Church, served in the 101st Regiment Infantry and was called the Fighting Chaplain of St. Michael's. Today, Veterans Post 2005 (below) is named for him. Also serving were Phanuel Covell, pastor of the First Baptist Church, 2nd Battalion Trench Motor, France; Thomas Mark, pastor at Base 6, Bensonhurst, Brooklyn, New York; and John Francis Monahan, assistant rector of the Star of the Sea Church, Medical Corps, Fort Oglethorpe, Georgia. (Courtesy Marblehead Historical Society.)

MARBLEHEAD'S CHAPLAINS

LYMAN ROLLINS
Rector St. Michael's Episcopal Church
Chaplain 101st Regiment Infantry, A. E. F.

PHANUEL B. COVELL
Pastor First Baptist Church
Chaplain 2nd Battalion Trench Motor, France

THOMAS M. MARK
Pastor Universalist Church
Chaplain, Base 6, Bensonhurst, Brooklyn, N. Y.

JOHN FRANCIS MONAHAN
Assistant Rector, Star of the Sea Church
Chaplain Medical Corps, Fort Oglethorpe, Georgia

The Gardner House on Gregory Street dates from 1636 and is one of the most photographed houses in town. Used first as a fish house on Marblehead Neck, the building was later moved by oxcart to its present location. (Courtesy Marblehead Historical Society.)

Redd's Pond, located at the end of Pond Street and abutting Old Burial Hill, has long left a mark on anyone who has sailed a model boat on it or skated on it during the winter. It was enlarged and turned into a reservoir in 1877 as part of an effort to increase the town's supply of fresh water. Boys of yesterday (below) sail their vessels with the aid of a stick. Today, their counterparts sail motorized versions on summer weekends. (Courtesy Marblehead Historical Society.)

Thanks to Uriel Crocker, residents and visitors alike have enjoyed Crocker Park, overlooking Marblehead Harbor. The view of the park has remained largely unchanged since the 1917 postcard (above) was sent. Uriel Crocker gave most of the land known as Bartoll's Head to the town in 1886. It was the first public park in Marblehead. Crocker, the man on the right, was photographed on his 90th birthday (September 13, 1886) with his business partner, Mr. Brewster. In business together for 75 years, Crocker and Brewster were book publishers. Their most successful book was a Bible in six volumes set up on copper stereotype plates. (Courtesy Marblehead Historical Society.)

Stacy H. Clark, a harbor master, has his name repeated often today, especially when speaking of patrols on the harbor. His name can be found on the harbor master's boat. The police department originally had the boat, as seen in the 1950s (below). Clark (far right) is shown on the docks *c.* 1900 with Jack Snow. In the background is the transportation building, built in the mid–18th century, one of the earliest remaining maritime structures. (Courtesy Marblehead Historical Society.)

The Herreshoff Castle (below), known as Castle Brattahlid when built in 1926 by designer Waldo Ballard (left), is at one entrance to Crocker Park. Complete with a dungeon, it was modeled after the ancient castle of Eric the Red of Greenland. Yacht designer L. Francis Herreshoff purchased it in 1945. Today, it is a private home and bed-and-breakfast establishment. (Courtesy Marblehead Historical Society.)

Marblehead has a proud tradition of open town meeting and a board of selectmen. In front of the original *Spirit of '76*, members of the board in 2000 (right) being sworn in by longtime town clerk Betty Brown are, from left to right, Diane St. Laurent, Judy Jacobi, Jeff Shribman, Bill Purdin, and William Woodfin II. You can be sure that the members of the 1902 board (below) never thought a woman would someday hold the same seat. They are, from left to right, Benjamin Cole, G.H. Thorburn, H.C. Sparhawk, town clerk W.T. Litchman, A.S. Ramsdell, and Richard Brown. (Below, courtesy Marblehead Historical Society; right, courtesy Selectmen's Office.)

The Devereux Mansion Sanatorium, founded by Dr. Herbert J. Hall, once stood on Beach Street and served as the home for the "nervously distressed." It was Herbert Hall who began Marblehead Pottery in 1904 as a therapeutic activity for his patients. The pieces are now most sought after by collectors of art pottery. In 1915, Arthur Baggs acquired the pottery operation and turned it into a full-fledged business at 111 Front Street. The kiln was located on Goodwin's Court. The business closed completely in 1940.

Dr. Herbert J. Hall (right) in September 1914 was the proprietor of the Devereux Mansion Sanatorium and founder of Marblehead Pottery as part of his Work Cure Program, which also included metalwork and other trades. Karen McGinnis (below), curator of collections for the Marblehead Historical Society, shows some of the Marblehead pottery owned by the Marblehead Historical Society. In its heyday, more than 200 pieces were produced per week. (Courtesy Marblehead Historical Society.)

Sam Bradish (front left), who served as police chief in the 1940s and 1950s, and motorcycle officer Norman "Peanut" Powers (right) pose outside the Old Town House with the crossing guards in the 1950s. The crossing guards are, from left to right, as follows: (front row) Barbara Williams, unidentified, and ? Gould; (back row) Mary Symonds, unidentified, Winona Doliber, Jane Kennerson, and Cathryn Hill. (Courtesy Marblehead Police Department.)

James Carney (right) was appointed police chief by the board of selectmen in 2000. Motorcycle officers Jack Percy (below left) and Bill Dennis pose with their trusty two-wheelers in 1964. (Courtesy Marblehead Police Department.)

The rights spelled out in the Declaration of Independence and fought for by many Marbleheaders in the Revolutionary War—life, liberty, and the pursuit of happiness—seem to have a newfound meaning after the terrorist attacks of September 11, 2001. Perhaps we thought for a moment that our town would not be touched directly by such a horrific event. As the day wore on, however, we learned that even this quiet seaside town would not escape the grief. In fact, Marblehead was one of the first towns in Massachusetts to hold a candlelight vigil. As the crowd gathered in the darkness of Seaside Park, the grandstand seemed to grieve, too. There would be no crowd cheering for the favorite American pastime. Instead, the crowd learned that three Marblehead men—Erik Isbrandtsen, Dr. Fredrick Rimmele III, and William Weems—had lost their lives in the attacks. The loss of these men has left a mark on Marblehead. This doorway on High Street is just an example of how these values are openly expressed in Marblehead. Coincidentally, this doorway is just across the street from where one of the victims of the World Trade Center tragedy had lived.